A Note from
Mary Pope Osborne About the

MAGIC TREE HOUSE® FACT TRACKERS

When I write Magic Tree House® adventures, I love including facts about the times and places Jack and Annie visit. But when readers finish these adventures, I want them to learn even more. So that's why we write a series of nonfiction books that are companions to the fiction titles in the Magic Tree House® series. We call these books Fact Trackers because we love to track the facts! Whether we're researching dinosaurs, pyramids, Pilgrims, sea monsters, or cobras, we're always amazed at how wondrous and surprising the real world is. We want you to experience the same wonder we do—so get out your pencils and notebooks and hit the trail with us. You can be a Magic Tree House® Fact Tracker, too!

Mary Pope Osborne

P9-DBY-427

Here's what kids, parents, and teachers have to say about the Magic Tree House® Fact Trackers:

"They are so good. I can't wait for the next one. All I can say for now is prepare to be amazed!" —Alexander N.

"I have read every Magic Tree House book there is. The [Fact Trackers] are a thrilling way to get more information about the special events in the story." —John R.

"These are fascinating nonfiction books that enhance the magical time-traveling adventures of Jack and Annie. I love these books, especially *American Revolution.* I was learning so much, and I didn't even know it!" —Tori Beth S.

"[They] are an excellent 'behind-the-scenes' look at what the [Magic Tree House fiction] has started in your imagination! You can't buy one without the other; they are such a complement to one another." —Erika N., mom

"Magic Tree House [Fact Trackers] took my children on a journey from Frog Creek, Pennsylvania, to so many significant historical events! The detailed manuals are a remarkable addition to the classic fiction Magic Tree House books we adore!" —Jenny S., mom

"[They] are very useful tools in my classroom, as they allow for students to be part of the planning process. Together, we find facts in the [Fact Trackers] to extend the learning introduced in the fictional companions. Researching and planning classroom activities, such as our class Olympics based on facts found in *Ancient Greece and the Olympics,* help create a genuine love for learning!" —Paula H., teacher

MAGIC TREE HOUSE® FACT TRACKER

NARWHALS AND OTHER WHALES

A NONFICTION COMPANION TO MAGIC TREE HOUSE #33:
Narwhal on a Sunny Night

BY MARY POPE OSBORNE AND NATALIE POPE BOYCE

ILLUSTRATED BY ISIDRE MONÉS

A STEPPING STONE BOOK™

Random House 🏠 New York

The Magic Tree House Fact Tracker series was formerly known as the Magic
Tree House Research Guide series.

Visit us on the Web!
MagicTreeHouse.com
rhcbooks.com

Educators and librarians, for a variety of teaching tools, visit us at
RHTeachersLibrarians.com

Library of Congress Cataloging-in-Publication Data
Names: Osborne, Mary Pope, author. | Boyce, Natalie Pope, author. | Monés,
Isidre, illustrator.
Title: Narwhals and other whales / by Mary Pope Osborne and Natalie Pope
Boyce; illustrated by Isidre Monés.
Description: New York: Random House, [2020] | Series: Magic Tree House Fact
Tracker; 42 | Audience: Age 7–10. | "A stepping stone book." | "A nonfiction
companion to Magic Tree House #33: narwhal on a sunny night."
Identifiers: LCCN 2019003026 | ISBN 978-1-9848-9320-8 (trade pbk.) |
ISBN 978-1-9848-9321-5 (lib. bdg.) | ISBN 978-1-9848-9322-2 (ebook)
Subjects: LCSH: Narwhal—Juvenile literature. | Whales—Juvenile literature.
Classification: LCC QL737.C433 O83 2020 | DDC 599.5/43—dc23

Printed in the United States of America

10 9 8 7 6 5 4 3 2 1

This book has been officially leveled by using the F&P Text Level Gradient™
Leveling System.

For Nathaniel Pope, with love

Scientific Consultant:

ANNALISA BERTA, PhD, Department of Biology, San Diego State
University

Education Consultant:

HEIDI JOHNSON, language acquisition and science education specialist,
Bisbee, Arizona

Special thanks to the Random House team: Mallory Loehr, Jenna Lettice,
Isidre Monés, Polo Orozco, Jason Zamajtuk, and especially to our beloved
editor, Diane Landolf

Narwhals and
Other Whales

Contents

Dear Readers,

When we came back from our adventure in <u>Narwhal on a Sunny Night</u>, we wanted to learn more about narwhals.

We found out narwhals are whales that live in the Arctic Ocean. For most of the year, the Arctic is a frozen world—even the ocean is frozen!

We watched videos of narwhals swimming in the freezing Arctic waters. The males have a tooth, or tusk, that sticks out of their mouth and can grow to be nine feet long!

Narwhals are such shy animals that scientists have a hard time studying

them. But in recent years, they've found out surprising things about these strange and wonderful creatures.

We were amazed to learn incredible facts about the Arctic Ocean and the beautiful animals that make it their home.

Jack

Annie

1

Narwhals and Other Whales

The Arctic is an icy region at the northern tip of the world. The Arctic Ocean, plus parts of Canada, Alaska, Russia, Greenland, Finland, Sweden, Denmark, Iceland, and Norway are all in the Arctic.

The Arctic is a beautiful, lonely place. For much of the year, it's battered by wind and covered in snow and ice. In spite of the brutal weather, narwhals and many other sea creatures thrive in the icy Arctic waters.

The North Pole is in the Arctic Ocean. It's an imaginary point marking the top of the world. There is no land at the North Pole, just masses of floating ice. In some spots, the ice is more than ten feet thick!

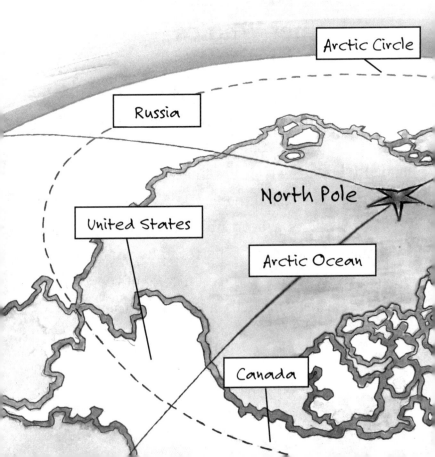

The Arctic Ocean

The Arctic Ocean is the smallest, shallowest, coldest ocean on earth. It covers five and a half million square miles. That's about one and a half times the size of the United States.

In the winter, floating ice jams the surface of the ocean. Icebergs, which are massive chunks of ice that have broken off from glaciers, drift through the water.

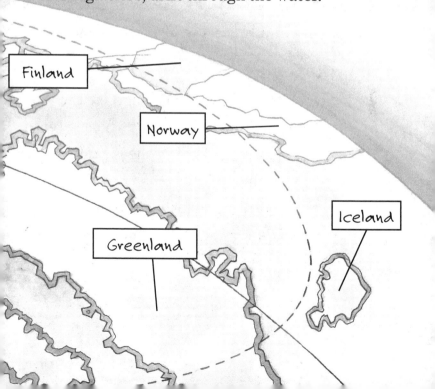

 Icebergs are made of fresh, not salty, water.

Icebergs may look huge on the surface, but you can see only about a tenth of the iceberg. Most of the gigantic piece of ice is underwater.

In 1912, people believed the cruise ship *Titanic* was so well built that it could never sink. But the ship rammed into an underwater section of an iceberg. It sank in less than three hours. Fifteen hundred people died in this terrible disaster.

The tallest iceberg ever found in the Arctic was off the coast of Greenland. It was as tall as the Washington Monument!

In the winter, temperatures in the Arctic average around minus 40 degrees Fahrenheit. During the summer, they rise to around 32 degrees. Then about half the sea ice melts, and plants and algae begin growing on land and in the water. They are food that many animals need to survive.

The coldest temperature on record in the Arctic is 70 degrees below zero off the coast of northern Greenland.

Polar Nights and Days

The coldest months in the Arctic are December through March. During this time,

17

the northern half of the earth tilts away from the sun, causing the Arctic to be dark all night . . . and all day as well! The opposite happens in spring and summer, as the North tilts toward the sun. Then the Arctic has twenty-four hours of daylight!

Because the sun never completely sets during the summer, the Arctic is called the Land of the Midnight Sun.

Well . . . how do we know when to go to bed?

Maybe we can just stay up all night!

Life in the Arctic

In spite of the Arctic's cold climate, people manage to live in these harsh and beautiful lands. It is also rich in animal and plant life.

The Arctic Ocean has more species of fish than any other ocean. Porpoises, walruses, and seals also thrive there. Narwhals and two other kinds of whales—bowheads and some belugas—live year

Walruses sometimes use their tusks to pull themselves up onto the ice.

round in its cold, dark waters. Polar bears hunt for prey on the ocean's frozen surface as seabirds swoop overhead.

Studying the Arctic Ocean

Researching life in the Arctic is a challenge for scientists. Because few people

 The ice is so thick, special ships called icebreakers must cut through the ice before other ships can pass.

live so far north, there are not many cities or airports nearby. Arctic researchers face lonely weeks of total darkness, deadly temperatures, and terrible storms.

Divers wear warm diving suits to protect themselves from freezing. There is always the danger that they will get trapped under the ice if it shifts and not be able to get out. They also have to stay alert for polar bears searching for food.

The best way to see life deep in the Arctic Ocean is with submarines. Satellites and special equipment placed on the ice also give scientists information. They can check on climate changes and the melting of the sea ice. Researchers have recently begun using drones that fly over the ice.

Studying the Arctic Ocean takes a lot of planning. Some scientists work in stations built right on the ice. They must

Waterproof backpack

Tent

Insulated rubber boots

Hiking boots

Hand and foot warmers

Sunglasses with straps

Padded rain jacket

Three-layer rain pants

Heavy socks

Fleece jacket

have snowmobiles, ice drills, and lots of research equipment, as well as food and medicine to last for months.

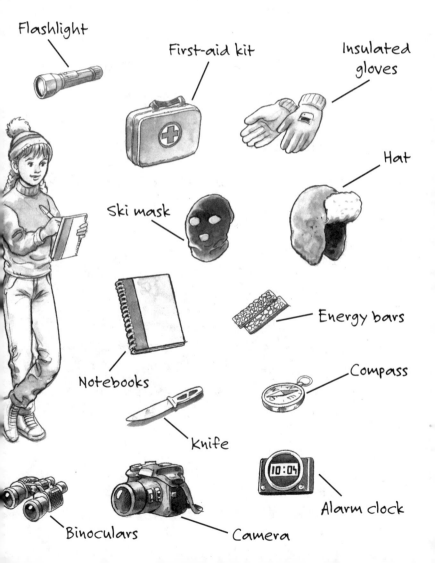

Flashlight

First-aid kit

Insulated gloves

Hat

Ski mask

Energy bars

Compass

Notebooks

Knife

Binoculars

Camera

Alarm clock

Why Don't Sea Creatures Freeze?

Narwhals and other whales have about the same body temperature as humans. But Arctic animals have ways of surviving the constant cold. Some, like Arctic codfish, have a chemical in their bodies that keeps them from freezing.

Some, like sea otters, have thick hair that keeps them warm. About 130,000

With thick layers of fur, sea otters have the thickest coats of any animal.

sea otter hairs grow in a spot the size of your fingertip. That's more hair than you have on your whole head!

Many animals in the Arctic Ocean trap heat in layers of fat called *blubber* that lie just under their skin. Walruses, for example, stay warm with the help of their super-thick skin plus thick blubber layers. Blubber also helps animals stay afloat in the water.

Even though scientists are learning more about narwhals and other Arctic animals, there are still many exciting discoveries ahead.

The giant lion's mane jellyfish lives in the Arctic Ocean and has stinging tentacles that can be over one hundred feet long!

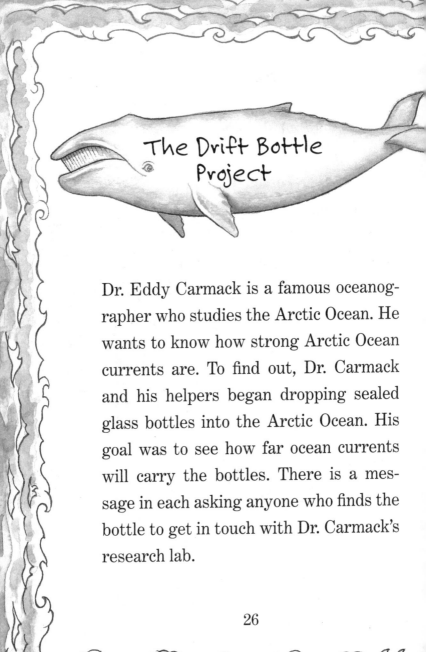

The Drift Bottle Project

Dr. Eddy Carmack is a famous oceanographer who studies the Arctic Ocean. He wants to know how strong Arctic Ocean currents are. To find out, Dr. Carmack and his helpers began dropping sealed glass bottles into the Arctic Ocean. His goal was to see how far ocean currents will carry the bottles. There is a message in each asking anyone who finds the bottle to get in touch with Dr. Carmack's research lab.

Since the project began, he's heard from people in places thousands of miles away, such as France, Norway, Spain, and Ireland!

2

Narwhals

Narwhals are whales that live off the coasts of Canada, Greenland, Russia, and Norway. They are strange and beautiful creatures with sleek bodies that can move easily through the water. Because narwhals don't survive in captivity, it's difficult for scientists to study them closely.

Narwhals are the only whales that have one long spiraled tusk. And because this

tusk looks like a unicorn horn, narwhals
are often called the "unicorns of the sea."

A Narwhal's Body
Male narwhals are medium-sized whales
between thirteen and eighteen feet long.
They can weigh over 3,500 pounds. Females weigh about 1,000 pounds less.

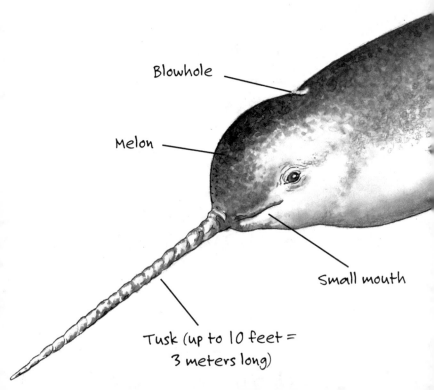

Blowhole

Melon

Small mouth

Tusk (up to 10 feet =
3 meters long)

Like all other whales, narwhals are mammals. They have lungs and breathe oxygen. They do this through a hole on top of their head called a *blowhole*. The whales swim to the surface and take in oxygen through their blowhole.

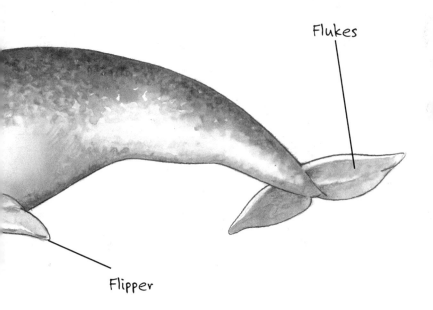

Flukes

Flipper

People can see a whale's spout from miles away.

When they spout, or exhale, the air shoots out of the blowhole in a misty spray.

Narwhal Migration

Twice a year, in the summer and fall, narwhals *migrate* from one part of the Arctic Ocean to another. They swim in groups

When animals **migrate**, they move from one place to another. Some travel great distances.

32

called *pods*. The pods hunt and swim together. There may be only a few narwhals in a pod or hundreds of them. Members of the pod connect with one another by making different kinds of sounds.

In the summer, narwhals live near the coast, where the water isn't extremely deep. They feed on cod, squid, halibut, and shrimp. Since narwhals don't have teeth to grab their prey, they suck food into their mouths like vacuum cleaners.

In the fall, ice near the shore begins to freeze into a solid mass. There are no open spaces where the narwhals can come up for air, so they head for deeper waters. Even though ice is thicker in very deep water, it has cracks in it. This gives the whales a place to breathe.

Narwhals are the only whales that spend all winter where the ice is thickest.

Young, Older, Oldest!

By studying the lens of a narwhal's eye, researchers can usually tell its age. Based on this, they think that narwhals can live to be ninety or even one hundred years old!

The color of a narwhal's skin is another

 Baby whales are called <u>calves</u>.

way to guess its age. Young narwhals are pale blue and gray. As they get older, their skin becomes darker and has dark spots on it. As time passes, the spots grow whiter. Old narwhals are totally white. To some people they seem like sea ghosts quietly gliding by.

The word *narwhal* comes from Viking words that mean "corpse whale." The Vikings thought this was the right name for a creature so pale that it looked dead!

Narwhal Tusks

A narwhal's tusk isn't a horn. It's actually a long spiral tooth that grows from its jaw through its upper lip. Narwhal calves are not born with a tusk . . . it grows as the calf gets older.

Narwhals have two teeth, but only the left one grows into a tusk.

Females usually don't have tusks. But a male's can grow to ten feet long and bend about a foot in any

Narwhal tusk

direction! If the tusk breaks, it never grows back.

Narwhals can swim upside down! They may do this to protect their tusks from scraping against something sharp on the ocean floor.

Elephants, hippos, wild pigs, and walruses have curved tusks. Narwhals are the only animals with straight ones.

A Tusk with Sensors?

Because narwhals are so hard to study, scientists aren't totally sure why they have tusks or all the ways they use them.

But researchers have recently discovered some interesting things about narwhal tusks. Human teeth are hard on the outside and softer on the inside. A narwhal's tusk is just the opposite. (Remember, the tusk is actually a tooth.) It has a soft outer layer filled with millions of nerve cells that connect to the narwhal's brain.

When an iceberg melts, it releases freshwater that makes water around it less salty.

Not all scientists agree on what these cells detect. Some think they sense conditions in the ocean such as the saltiness of the water. A narwhal's heart beats faster in salt water and slows down in less salty water.

Another possibility is that during mating season, a male uses his tusk to sense any females that might be in the area. Or the tusks may attract females.

Male and female narwhals usually mate between March and May.

Male narwhals often touch one another's tusks. Since they don't fight with their tusks, this may be a way of communicating or connecting.

As the males touch tusks, they make whistling sounds.

Tusks for Smacking Cod?

Researchers learned something exciting recently. Two drones flying off the coast of Canada recorded narwhals smacking codfish with their tusks. The fish were so stunned that they couldn't move, giving the narwhals a chance to eat them. This was the first time scientists had ever seen this behavior.

Echolocation

Narwhals can sense what's in the ocean's dark waters by using *echolocation* (eh-koh-loh-KAY-shun). Echolocation is when animals use echoes from the sounds they make to locate objects around them.

Bats, porpoises, and some other whales use echolocation, too.

Narwhals often swim in water so deep that there is no light to see. They solve this problem by making clicking

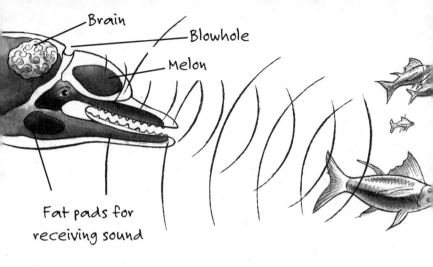

Brain

Blowhole

Melon

Fat pads for receiving sound

sounds . . . sometimes as many as 1,000 each second! The sounds are so high that human ears can't hear them.

As the whales make these noises, a round, fatty organ on their head called a *melon* directs the sound out into the water.

The echoes bounce back to the narwhals, giving them a "sound" picture of what's in the water. They can find food and communicate with other narwhals by listening to their own echo!

Diving

In order to search for cod and other fish, narwhals often dive deep into the ocean. Sometimes they swim down more than a mile!

When they dive, they close their blow-holes to keep the water out. Sometimes

For six months of the year, narwhals make deep dives between eighteen and twenty times a day!

they remain below the surface for as long as twenty-five minutes.

They are able to stay down for so long because of the high oxygen levels in their blood and muscles. They also gain extra oxygen by cutting the blood flow to other parts of their body.

Narwhals Help Out

Oceanographers wanted to find more about changes in the ice around Greenland. Someone came up with the idea that narwhals might be helpful.

Because narwhals are very shy creatures, scientists rarely see them. They were able, however, to trap some off the coast of Greenland. The researchers managed to attach sensors to the backs of fourteen narwhals.

Scientists tagging a narwhal

As the narwhals swam through the water, the sensors sent back information about the temperature, the saltiness of the water, and changes to the ice.

One scientist later said that even though narwhals are shy and hard to find, they are very good at collecting information! With the help of modern science, researchers are learning a lot more about these wild and unusual creatures.

45

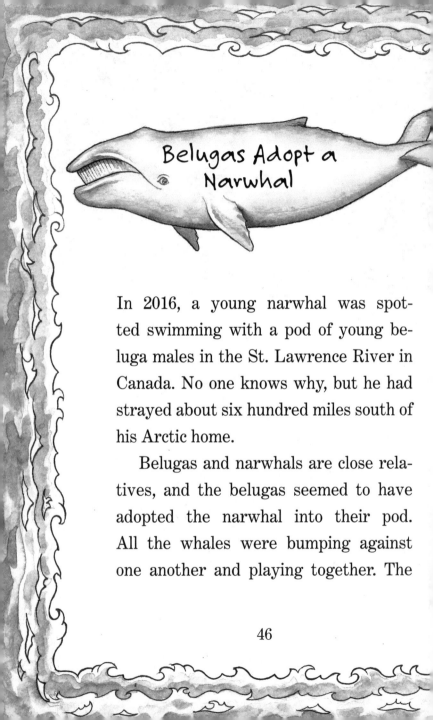

Belugas Adopt a Narwhal

In 2016, a young narwhal was spotted swimming with a pod of young beluga males in the St. Lawrence River in Canada. No one knows why, but he had strayed about six hundred miles south of his Arctic home.

Belugas and narwhals are close relatives, and the belugas seemed to have adopted the narwhal into their pod. All the whales were bumping against one another and playing together. The narwhal even started blowing bubbles like his beluga pals! As of 2018, the narwhal was still swimming with the belugas.

3

Narwhals and Myths

The Inuit people of Greenland, Canada, and Alaska have lived around narwhals longer than anyone else. For at least a thousand years, they have hunted them for their meat, blubber, and tusks.

Knud Rasmussen, who lived around one hundred years ago, is one of the most famous early Arctic explorers. Knud's father was a Danish missionary in Greenland.

His mother was part Danish, part Inuit. Knud spent his early years in Greenland playing with Inuit kids and learning their language.

Even though his family moved to Denmark, Knud was fascinated with the Arctic. At that time, few besides the native Arctic people knew much about it.

 Knud wrote a book called <u>The People of the Polar North</u>.

Knud was one of the first Europeans to explore Greenland and the Arctic. He traveled long distances on a dogsled to learn more about the Arctic. Knud watched as the Inuit hunted narwhals and went about their everyday life. He used the notes he took on his trips to write books about his explorations.

Inuit and Narwhals

Narwhal blubber was, and still is, an important part of the Inuit diet. It is loaded with vitamin C, which prevents a deadly disease called scurvy.

In the Inuit language a narwhal is called "the one who points to the sky." During his travels, Knud heard Inuit myths and songs that he wrote down.

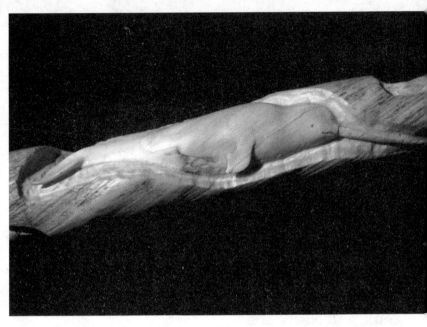

The Inuit carved spear points and knives as well as images of animals and people out of narwhal tusks.

One of the most famous Inuit myths is about an Inuit woman who was hunting a whale with a harpoon connected to a rope. Her son tied the rope around her waist and then hurled the harpoon at the whale. The harpoon hit the whale and it moved out to the safety of the sea. The woman was pulled into the water.

As she sank down deep, her body turned into a narwhal's body. Her long braid whipped round and round until it became the narwhal's famous tusk.

Narwhal or Unicorn?

You do know that unicorns are not real animals, right? These magical horses with a single horn are myths, but people who lived two thousand years ago believed them to be real. Unicorn myths

began to spread all over China, the Middle East, and Europe.

The Vikings realized that narwhal tusks looked like unicorn horns. They figured out that if they sold narwhal tusks as unicorn horns, they could make a lot of money. The Vikings became the most active traders of fake unicorn horns, selling them in England and throughout Europe.

Vikings may have traded with the Inuit to get the first narwhal tusks.

Unicorn Horn Madness!

The tusks were so rare that they cost a huge amount of money. Some rich people wanted a unicorn horn—or two, or three!

In 1577, an English explorer named Martin Frobisher sailed home from the coast of Canada with a narwhal tusk he'd come across. He presented it to Queen

Elizabeth I and told her it was a unicorn's horn. The queen gave Martin a lot of money for it—about the price of a castle!

Rulers also gave narwhal horns as gifts to people they wanted to impress.

Kings and bishops carried staffs made from narwhal tusks. In the late 1400s, Charles the Bold, the Duke of Burgundy in France, had a sword made of a narwhal's tusk. And the Austrian Court stored their precious horns in treasure houses along with their jewels and other riches.

Charles the Bold

Horns Cure Disease!

People believed the tusks had special powers. They thought unicorn horns could protect them from disease. Doctors ground up the tusks and called it unicorn powder. They promised it could cure everything from colds to rabid dog bites! Not true!

A "unicorn" cup made from
a narwhal's tusk.

Powerful people often worried that
enemies were plotting to poison them.
To be sure that a drink was safe, they
poured liquid into a cup made from a
"unicorn" horn.

If the liquid foamed, they thought it was proof that someone had put poison in their cup! (Yikes!) But then they also believed the horns made the poison harmless, so they could drink all they wanted!

Museums sometimes have medieval ancient tapestries, or wall hangings, like this one, in their collection.

By the 1700s, people knew more about the world and realized that unicorns were not real animals. Queen Elizabeth would have been so angry to learn that her precious unicorn horn actually came from the tusk of a whale that swam in the icy Arctic Ocean!

Turn the page to find out about an amazing narwhal throne!

The Most Splendid Throne

A throne is a special chair where kings used to sit during special events. Denmark's king had one of the most famous thrones of all. It's now in the Great Hall of Rosenborg Castle.

Craftsmen built it in the 1600s when people thought unicorns were real. The great white throne has legs made of narwhal tusks that were supposed to be unicorn horns. Three life-sized silver lions stand around the throne. The lions' eyes, made of pure gold, never blink as they stand guard over the Danes' magical unicorn throne.

Narwhal tusks

4

Whales Living in
Arctic Waters

There are two main kinds of whale: toothed and baleen.

Baleen whales have special filters in their mouths called *baleen plates*. The plates have keratin bristles on them like a brush. They trap small organisms for the whales to eat.

Baleen whales are the largest whales and have two blowholes for all the oxygen

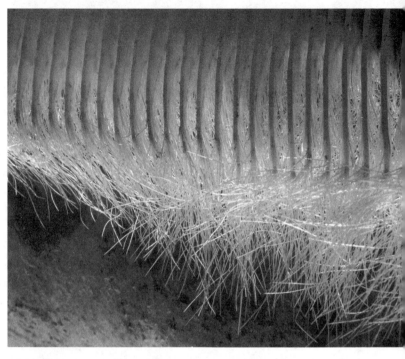

 Your fingernails and hair are also made of keratin.

their bodies need. They eat tons of very small animals, including *krill*.

Water filled with krill and other creatures pours into the whale's mouth. The whale closes its baleen plates, forcing the water out and leaving the tiny animals trapped in the baleen hairs.

Most whales have teeth and use them to attack their prey and swallow it whole.

Seventeen species of whale swim in the Arctic Ocean. Some stay all year. Others spend summers there and then migrate to warmer waters in the late fall.

Krill are tiny shrimplike animals that are only about an inch long.

Belugas

Belugas are toothed whales that live in the Arctic and in cold waters just south of the Arctic near Russia, Greenland, and Alaska. In the summer, they often stay near the coast where the water is shallow. When the ocean begins to freeze, belugas migrate south.

Young belugas are gray or brown until they are about five years old. Then they begin turning white or light gray. Their pale bodies blend in well with the Arctic ice. The word *beluga* comes from a Russian word meaning "white."

Belugas are smaller whales—about fifteen feet long. They have round bodies

Beluga

and no back fins. The large bulging melon on their head changes shape when the whales make different sounds.

Blubber makes up almost half of a beluga's weight. Bowheads are the only whales that have more blubber than belugas.

Polar bears need blubber in their diet, so belugas are one of their favorite foods.

Unlike other whales, belugas can turn their heads from side to side as well as up and down. And they can also swim backward! This helps them avoid predators, like killer whales and polar bears. Belugas can move their mouths into different shapes to suck up fish from the ocean floor.

Being Together
Belugas almost always live in pods of about ten to twelve whales. The

70

Belugas sometimes blow bubble rings for fun.

strongest male usually leads the group. Females look out for one another's calves, or babies.

The group hunts and migrates together. During a migration, different pods often join together. At times, as many as 1,000 whales swim in one huge, amazing pod!

Sea Canaries

Early sailors called belugas *sea canaries* because they can make so many different sounds. They do this to communicate with one another. Researchers have heard them mew, bleat, chirp, cheep, cluck, click, and whistle!

Unlike narwhals, belugas do well in captivity and seem comfortable around humans. They sometimes imitate the human sounds around them.

In 1984, Navy researchers were working with captive belugas. They hoped the belugas' echolocation skills could help find unexploded torpedoes at the bottom of the sea.

They noticed that one of the whales, named NOC (NO-see), had begun making human sounds. Once, they heard some-

Captive belugas sometimes spit streams of water!

one yell "OUT!" The diver thought it was his boss telling him it was time to get out of the water. It wasn't his boss . . . it was NOC!

Bowhead Whales

Like narwhals, bowhead whales live in the Arctic all year. Imagine an animal

73

almost as long as two school buses and weighing over 200,000 pounds. That's about 100 tons! Bowheads keep growing until they are about fifty years old! (You grow until you're about sixteen.)

These slow-moving baleen whales are mostly black, with white or gray around

their jaws. Their massive heads make up about a third of their entire body.

Bowheads get their name because their mouths curve like an archery bow. They have more blubber than any other whale. In addition, bowheads have incredibly thick skulls. When these giant

 Scientists can tell one bowhead from another by their scars from breaking through the ice.

animals need to breathe and can't find a crack in the ice, they can smash their heads right through eight inches or more of ice to get air!

The Biggest Mouth

Everything about a bowhead is huge. They have the biggest mouth of any animal on the planet. They need it because they eat about two tons of food every day! In fact, their tongue alone weighs over a ton! There is a series of baleen plates on either side of their upper jaws with about 250 to 350 bristles in each.

Bowheads can feed under thick ice.

The bowhead mainly eats krill. It gathers food by swimming slowly all day with its mouth wide open. It closes its mouth and then pushes the water out, leaving the krill behind, trapped in the baleen bristles.

Behavior

From November until April when the weather is at its coldest, males make different noises that sound a lot like songs. The more frozen the ice gets, the more they sing. At times, they sing all day and all night without stopping!

Ancient Giants

Scientists have found old harpoon points in the bodies of some bowheads. People only hunted with points like these in the 1800s. This proves that these whales can live for over one hundred years!

By studying its eyes, scientists have discovered one bowhead that was at least 211 years old when it died!

Bowhead whales are fascinating animals that can do things no other animals can do. They sing for months without stopping, bash holes through thick ice with their heads, and live longer than any mammal!

Like many other whales, bowheads often leap high out of the water. This is called <u>breaching</u>.

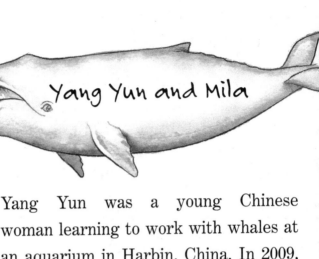

Yang Yun and Mila

Yang Yun was a young Chinese woman learning to work with whales at an aquarium in Harbin, China. In 2009, she and some other students tried to see how long they could hold their breath underwater.

There were some beluga whales in the tank with them. The water was twenty feet deep and icy cold. Yun began to have terrible leg cramps. She found it impossible to move her legs and started to sink to the bottom. She knew she was in serious trouble when she couldn't get any air and began to swallow water and choke.

Suddenly there was a strong force pushing her up to the surface. It was Mila, one of the belugas! She had Yun's leg in her mouth! People watching were stunned as Mila pushed Yun up to safety. She was saved by a whale!

5

Other Whales
in the Arctic

Whales are the largest mammals in the world. Because oceans cover about 70 percent of the planet, these huge animals have plenty of room to move around.

At certain times of the year, many whales migrate long distances from one part of the ocean to another. During the year, seventeen species of whale swim in the Arctic Ocean. Narwhals, bowheads, and some groups of belugas are the only ones living there year round.

Other species spend only part of the year in the Arctic. Their bodies can't survive the severe Arctic winters. As the weather gets colder, they swim to warmer waters where they can eat and have their calves.

Migration

In the late fall many whales, such as gray and humpback whales, leave the Arctic and head south. They return to the Arctic when the weather gets warmer and there is a good supply of food.

Some whales travel very long distances to their winter homes. Humpbacks, for example, swim thousands of miles between their winter and summer feeding grounds. They move slowly, not more than five miles per hour.

Finding Their Way

Scientists have studied migrating whales to find out how they find their way in the vast dark ocean. Many think that they sing to keep in touch with one another and to figure out where they are. The sounds they make send back images that act almost like a map.

There is also evidence that whales and other migrating animals have a built-in magnetic sense that lets them know the direction they need to take.

Whales sometimes heave their large bodies out of the water and look around as if they are trying to spot a landmark.

Spyhopping

This is called *spyhopping*. Researchers have noticed that gray whales sometimes do this near oil rigs. It's possible the rigs give them a clue about where they're going!

Now let's go and meet some other great Arctic whales!

Humpback Whale

Humpback whales are huge gray animals that weigh up to 80,000 pounds and are forty to fifty feet long. They get their name because they hump their backs up when they dive.

Humpbacks spend summers at the North and South Poles. Then they head to warmer waters in places like Mexico

and Hawaii. They don't eat all winter and survive on the fat stored in their bodies.

Humpbacks swim the longest distance of all whales. They cover about 16,000 miles going back and forth between their summer and winter homes. They sing as they swim. Their songs might be heard many miles away!

Humpbacks can go four months without food.

Gray Whale

Gray whales migrate from the Arctic down to Baja California, Mexico. They swim for two to three months and travel 6,000 miles without appearing to sleep!

These whales grow up to thirty-nine feet long and weigh up to 60,000 pounds.

Like cats, they have whiskers. The whiskers give them clues about what is happening around them.

When gray whales spray out their blowholes, water shoots up about thirteen feet in the air. The sound from it travels about a half mile!

Blue Whale

Blue whales live at the North and South Poles in the summer and in warmer waters in the winter. They are the largest creatures ever to have lived on earth and can be up to 100 feet long and weigh about 300,000 pounds!

Their heart alone weighs about 1,000 pounds . . . that's the size of a small car!

And their tongue is as heavy as an elephant! Isn't it amazing that these animals feed on sea creatures the size of your fingernail?

Blue whales are one of the loudest animals on the planet. When one makes noise, the sound travels miles through the water. It's louder than a jet engine!

Orca

Orca or killer whales are related to dolphins. They can be up to twenty-six feet long and weigh 12,000 pounds. Their backs are black, while their undersides are white. Orcas live in pods of up to forty whales. Each pod has a special sound so the whales can recognize other pod members. The pods may stay together for life.

Orcas eat about 500 pounds of food a day! Their diet includes fish, seals, penguins, squid, sharks, and other whales.

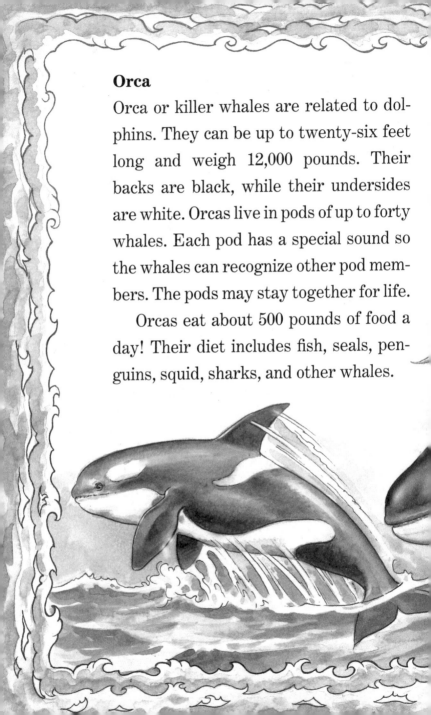

Since orcas swim at almost thirty miles an hour, they move in quickly on their prey.

When penguins or seals are on the ice, the whales smack the water with their tails. Waves wash their prey off into the ocean . . . and into their mouth! No animals except humans are a danger to the fierce killer whale.

Fin Whale

While blue whales are the largest whales, fin whales come in second. These giant baleen whales can grow up to sixty-eight feet long and weigh 100,000 pounds! In spite of their huge size, they are able to swim eighteen miles per hour, and for short distances they can speed up to twenty-three miles per hour. That's slow for a car, but really fast for an animal as long as two telephone poles!

Fin whales live in all the major oceans. Since they stay in deep water away from the shore, scientists have had a hard time learning about them.

Minke Whale

Minke (MIN-kuh) whales are one of the smallest of all the baleen whales. They grow to be up to thirty-five feet long and weigh up to 20,000 pounds. Minke live around the world. Many spend their summer in the Arctic.

Minkes seem to be curious about boats. They'll swim right up to them and circle around and around before they swim away. They also spyhop to look at the people on board. Sometimes they'll stay near a boat for a while before disappearing back into the ocean.

Some people have named these whales Stinky Minkes! That's because when they spout, the air that shoots up smells awful!

6

The Past and a Future

For centuries the Inuit have been amazing hunters on land and sea. Thousands of years ago, they began taking small boats out to hunt seals, whales, and walruses.

The Inuit had many important uses for these animals. They melted blubber for oil to burn in lamps. They ate the meat and turned the bones into useful things like cups, knives, and spears.

Experts think that the earliest hunters would surround a whale with their boats and run it up on shore. Later, they hunted whales by throwing or shooting harpoons at them. The harpoons had ropes attached.

Whaling in the 1800s

By the mid-1800s in America, Iceland, Norway, and Japan, whaling had become a big business. Ships loaded with whaling equipment sailed off for trips all over the world.

Small villages up and down the coast of New England depended on whaling to survive.

Whaling was a dangerous job. Sailors left their families and were often gone for a long time. People at home never

This 1880s illustration shows ship repairs in New Bedford, Massachusetts, which was once the busiest whaling seaport in the United States.

knew when their loved ones would return. They might be gone for months or even years.

Many whalers died from drowning, sickness, or accidents. Ships went through terrible storms and sank beneath the pounding waves. The sailors' families might not ever find out what had happened. Some people never lost hope that their loved ones would someday return.

Whale Products in the 1800s

Native people in the Arctic depended on whales for food and oil. But there was also a growing demand for whale oil in factories in the United States and England. Machines in factories needed oil. Some experts say that in the 1800s, more than 236,000 whales were killed for different uses.

Perfumes and Corsets

Women in the 1800s wore perfume made from a sticky substance called ambergris. It makes the smell of the perfume last longer. Ambergris comes from sperm whales' intestines!

To protect sperm whales today, there's a law in the United States against the use of ambergris.

Plastic wasn't invented until the early 1900s. Instead, people used teeth and baleen that came from the jaws of

105

some whales. It was called *whalebone*. People put it inside men's collars to make them stand up and made buggy whips and toys from it.

Chess pieces made from whale teeth

At this time, many women wore special underclothes called *corsets*, made from whalebone. They laced the corsets very tight to make their waists look small.

When people began pumping oil from under the ground, it took the place of whale oil, and the whaling industry began to shut down. Today,

Whalebone corset

whale hunting is allowed only in Japan, Iceland, and Norway. There are laws about the number of whales that can be killed each year.

Climate Change

The earth is getting warmer. Because of this, the Arctic is changing faster than any other place on the planet. As the Arctic Ocean gets warmer, ice is melting at a rapid rate. What will happen to animals like narwhals that thrive in icy weather if their world gets warmer and the sea ice begins to disappear? Climate change will definitely affect the future of wildlife in the Arctic and all over the world.

Scientists and conservation groups are working to protect the Arctic and its animals. These groups are teaming up with governments and native peoples to find ways to keep life in the Arctic healthy. They all agree that the Arctic and its incredible animals are gifts we must never lose.

Doing More Research

There's a lot more you can learn about narwhals and other whales. The fun of research is seeing how many different sources you can explore.

Books

Most libraries and bookstores have books about whales, including narwhals.

Here are some things to remember when you're using books for research:

1. You don't have to read the whole book. Check the table of contents and the index to find the topics you're interested in.

2. Write down the name of the book.

When you take notes, make sure you write down the name of the book in your notebook so you can find it again.

3. Never copy exactly from a book.

When you learn something new from a book, put it in your own words.

4. Make sure the book is <u>nonfiction</u>.

Some books tell make-believe stories about narwhals, other whales, and the Arctic. Make-believe stories are called *fiction*. They're fun to read, but not good for research.

Research books have facts and tell true stories. They are called *nonfiction*. A librarian or teacher can help you make sure the books you use for research are nonfiction.

Here are some good nonfiction books about narwhals and the Arctic:

- *Amazing Animals: Narwhals* by Logan Avery
- *Amazing Arctic Animals* by Jackie Glassman
- *Living in the Arctic* by Allan Fowler
- *Narwhal* (A Day in the Life: Polar Animals) by Katie Marsico
- *Narwhal: Revealing an Artic Legend* edited by Will Fitzhugh
- *Narwhal: Unicorn of the Sea* (Smithsonian Oceanic Collection) by Janet Halfmann
- *North: The Amazing Story of Arctic Migration* by Nick Dowson

Museums and Aquariums

Many museums and aquariums can help you learn more about narwhals and whales.

When you go to a museum or aquarium:

1. Be sure to take your notebook!
Write down anything that catches your interest. Draw pictures, too!

2. Ask questions.
There are almost always people at aquariums who can help you find what you're looking for.

3. Check the calendar.
Many aquariums have special events and activities just for kids!

Here are some museums and aquariums where you can learn about narwhals, other whales, and the Arctic:

- Columbus Zoo and Aquarium (Powell, Ohio)
- Dallas World Aquarium
- Georgia Aquarium (Atlanta)
- Monterey Bay Aquarium (Monterey, California)
- National Aquarium (Baltimore)
- New Bedford Whaling Museum (New Bedford, Massachusetts)
- New England Aquarium (Boston)
- Peary-MacMillan Arctic Museum (Brunswick, Maine)

The Internet

Many websites have lots of facts about narwhals, other whales, and the Arctic. Some also have activities that can help make learning about narwhals easier.

Ask your teacher or your parents to help you find more websites like these:

- a-z-animals.com/animals/location/ocean/
- enchantedlearning.com/coloring /arcticanimals.shtml
- enchantedlearning.com/subjects/whales /species/Narwhal.shtml
- kids.kiddle.co/Arctic
- kidsplayandcreate.com/unicorns-of-the -sea-narwhal-facts-for-kids/

- kids-world-travel-guide.com /arctic-ocean-facts.html

- natgeokids.com/za/discover/geography /general . . . /ten-facts-about-the-arctic/

- scienceforkidsclub.com/arctic.html

- study.com/academy/lesson/arctic -ocean-facts-lesson-for-kids.html

- whale-world.com/facts-about-whales -for-kids/

Bibliography

Gertner, Jon. *The Ice at the End of the World.* New York: Random House, 2019.

Herbert, Sir Wally, and Huw Lewis-Jones. *Across the Arctic Ocean.* New York: Thames & Hudson, 2015.

Lavers, Chris. *The Natural History of Unicorns.* New York: William Morrow, 2009.

Leatherwood, Stephen. *Whales, Dolphins, and Porpoises of the Eastern North Pacific and Adjacent Arctic Waters: A Guide to Their Identification.* New York: Dover Publications, 1988.

Lopez, Barry. *Arctic Dreams.* New York: Vintage Books, 2001.

McLeish, Todd. *Narwhals: Arctic Whales in a Melting World.* Seattle: University of Washington Press, 2013.

Paine, Stefani. *The World of the Arctic Whales: Belugas, Bowheads, and Narwhals.* San Francisco: Sierra Club Books, 1995.

Rasmussen, Knud. *Across Arctic America: Narrative of the Fifth Thule Expedition.* Fairbanks: University of Alaska Press, 1999.

Wheeler, Sara. *The Magnetic North: Notes from the Arctic Circle.* New York: Farrar, Straus and Giroux, 2011.

Index

*Have you read the adventure that
matches up with this book?*

Don't miss
Magic Tree House® #33

Narwhal on a Sunny Night

When the magic tree house whisks
Jack and Annie to Greenland, they're not
sure what time they've landed in. But they
do know this: there's a narwhal in trouble,
and they need to save it!

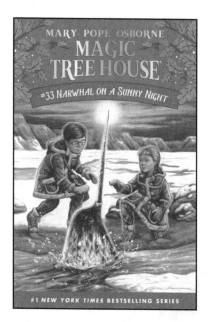

Magic Tree House®

Magic Tree House® Merlin Missions

Magic Tree House®
Super Edition

#1: World at War, 1944

Magic Tree House®
Fact Trackers

Dinosaurs

Knights and Castles

Mummies and Pyramids

Pirates

Rain Forests

Space

Titanic

Twisters and Other Terrible Storms

Dolphins and Sharks

Ancient Greece and the Olympics

American Revolution

Sabertooths and the Ice Age

Pilgrims

Ancient Rome and Pompeii

Tsunamis and Other Natural Disasters

Polar Bears and the Arctic

Sea Monsters

Penguins and Antarctica

Leonardo da Vinci

Ghosts

Leprechauns and Irish Folklore

Rags and Riches: Kids in the Time of Charles Dickens

Snakes and Other Reptiles

Dog Heroes

Abraham Lincoln

Pandas and Other Endangered Species

Horse Heroes

Heroes for All Times

Soccer

Ninjas and Samurai

China: Land of the Emperor's Great Wall

Sharks and Other Predators

Vikings

Dogsledding and Extreme Sports

Dragons and Mythical Creatures

World War II

Baseball

Wild West

Texas

Warriors

Benjamin Franklin

Narwhals and Other Whales

More Magic Tree House®

Games and Puzzles from the Tree House

Magic Tricks from the Tree House

My Magic Tree House Journal

Magic Tree House Survival Guide

Animal Games and Puzzles

Magic Tree House Incredible Fact Book